3

Contents

9

Foreword

I've seen signs in pubs that say: "beer is cheaper than therapy". For me, "poetry is cheaper than therapy" would be a more appropriate phrase (and, if you're drinking in London, it's probably also cheaper than beer). I am scared to share some of these poems because of their personal nature. Yet that same fear also spurs me on, bringing with it the exhilarating promise of deeper human connection made possible through risking vulnerability. Throughout my life, reading and writing poetry has enabled me to explore others' internal realities and find points of overlap with mine. Sometimes, it feels like the desire to "succeed" as a creative, or to amass a live and digital audience, detracts from the raw process of writing – its joy, its urgency. Through sharing my writings on the highs and lows of love, lust and romance, I wish to return to that core, emotionally connective function of literature, and to resonate with you in a way that opens up shared breathing space within life's lonelier moments.

All of your colours

Red is a passionate cliché
lipstick I smudged to my mouth
before meeting you at the pub –
not too much, just a touch –
such a delicate press of fingers on skin.

Orange is sunlight in the autumn afternoon
amber wood of a guitar body
and piles of leaves, wet with dew
by the side of the park path
passed in thoughts of change;

Yellow is both optimism and envy,
the rush of hope at the beginning
moment of winning your smile
bathed in light,
heart swelling like it would burst
in a sense-inflicted sunshine…

Green is grass-blades on Hampstead Heath and of North

English fields,

interior walling of vegan restaurants,

a t-shirt worn to sleep in,

the cover of reusable coffee cups.

Blue is inner peace and a winter sky

ink starting to chart an unwritten page

waves of an ocean mosaic hung up in my room.

Tranquillity, expansiveness,

a sea held from green eyes to blue ones,

sapphire hum of the open road leading nowhere.

Do we dare to venture here?

Indigo is evening, lonelier alone

wrapping my arms around myself to stay warm

between the shadows of Camden canal and the River Wear

dark covers of old novels

and storm of your absence,

a silent searching space

where dream-remnants cling to the day like cobwebs.

Violet is beauty

flooding through me and beyond me

I close my eyes and am overwhelmed by purple

energy in lilting jazz notes,

chords of a favourite song wordlessly picking strings of the

heart

bliss,

magic over the shades of everyday:

spiritual crescendo of a page read in your voice,

glow of your presence

like amethyst protection.

Our glances can only hint;

Poems cast their candles,

mauve lights glint

dissolving into the silver lining

of an indescribable feeling.

Insert to fill

I (gaze/ grimace/ glance)

down time's path towards a memory

of (sitting/ resting/ waiting) with you in the sunlight.

It was (summer/ autumn/ early spring) and the warmth

from (your meditations / my coffee) danced like (fireflies/ static/

birdsong)

around the bubble in our lives

that was meeting this (morning/ midday/ afternoon) somewhere

familiar.

Talking about (uni/ work/ pub nights) and un-tested political

ideologies (thrust/ beamed/ worn) in youthful conviction.

People we fancied. Past dates. Common (threads/ friends/

documentaries).

There was (so much/ nothing) to say.

And enough elastic in our timetables to stay.

I breathe like a (baby first meeting the world/ deep sea diver on

dwindling oxygen)

into the fabric of remembering.

Because this fragment reeks like a (sepia/ black and white/ low-

fi) filter

of how things were before,

and nothing about its normality

is normal anymore.

You take my (hesitations) out and fill in the gaps

while we talked, un-masked, unsteady

before the world moved to collapse.

Ellie, 24

This year I want to...

~~get a job I actually like, or at the very least find bearable. Reduce my~~
~~dosage of antidepressants.~~
travel – India or Bali?? X

Believe it or not, I...

~~haven't washed my hair for a week.~~
spoke on BBC radio last year.

Dating me is like...

~~being dragged down the motorway backwards.~~
sipping an espresso martini.

Honeymoon phase

I love you with pangs: your dark halo of hair;

your smile, and how I miss you when you're not there.

Your eyes catch the sunlight like two kind, brown lakes.

I want to hold hands with your heart, kiss the parts where it

aches.

I know you feel the chaos of a world that's so strange,

and get scared of death and the things you can't change.

But there's so much you give just by being alive,

both on days where you're glowing and when you struggle to

thrive.

Sometimes I get worried about you, drifting like an Autumn

leaf,

when you seem closed off and weighed down by grief

as you live on each impulse: changing colours, caught on

breezes,

trying to hold permanence in each of our hugs' squeezes.

I know you'll be fine, because all seasons shift

and your soul's light will shine to give others a lift.

And I'm here in the meantime as this journey unfolds,

You were never one colour but a rainbow of auburns, crimsons,

and golds.

I cannot give you everything, because I get scared too,

neither of us fully formed – merely muddling through.

I've spent fair time doubting, not knowing the road,

brain so overwhelmed that it's soon to explode,

but your presence warms me like a hot mug of tea

anchoring each other as Earth tilts degree by degree.

Love in 2021

Are you taking me for granted?

A metre yet a million miles away,

eyes slanted, brow furrowed,

you're burrowed deep into the world of your phone,

near me – in theory – but mind coasting somewhere far away

its cogs spinning, concocting character-tight repartee

to hurl into the frothing digital fray

with distant dreams of winning adulation in the Instagram

memes and Tik Tok Twitter sphere.

Baby, can you hear me? Can you hear me?

I'm right here

and beginning to get weary of it taking you

thirty seconds or longer to register things I say,

while trying to remain calm.

I love you. You love me too, right?

I know you do, but you're looking through this room, past the

dead weight of my arm

Blinded by blue light,

its rectangular seduction stuck to your palm

Like a permanent extension

Triggering dopamine hits through latest article mentions

Algorithms against which I'm ever in a losing battle to hold

your attention.

They're one up on me 'til I say something new

Or think of something for us to go out and do

But all I can offer are the maze and caverns of human

imperfection – my thoughts.

I don't come with celebrity reactions or up-to-date scores on

sports

or accurate meteorological projections.

And while I admire your tenacity

and seemingly bottomless capacity to use

your platform to call to action public support

for the rights of the exploited and poor, the souls whom UK

border force deports,

I'm all too aware that you are only half there,

staring into a mirror which distorts.

Our bodies are still built to crave partners

yet we reach for our Apple Galaxy Samsung 4G companions

rather than their hands

when we find ourselves in sleepless darkness;

livestreams, instant reels, what's fake, what's real, it's all gotten

too much.

And it isn't my soap-smelling naked skin but android pixels

that you're itching to touch.

And I somehow just can't shake it: this suspicion that still sticks

that I appealed more to you

when I was a pair of grey ticks

waiting to turn blue.

Hablar en Spanglish

To miss or to need

is *faltar*, like I falter

like I fall to the floor of the ocean, sunk to a place that's defined

by its lack.

But still dare to dream: *soñar*

Y echar palabras - throwing words – like sonar beamed

underwater

but I guess their sound's unheard

because you're not coming back.

Poesía, como rosas, como flores,

poems like a posy of flowers

lullabies lulling me to our cosy hours

navegando el mar; co-navigating like a pair of submarine

explorers.

Now I'm combing the wreckage of this *historia compartida* –

that's all our shared stories –

and I don't know where you are, can't see which way the shore
is,

not lit by your star.

I know there's a sky full of *otras estrellas*
And time's moving forwards, a one-way conveyer,
That tides have their own minds, not set to obey us,
that life is not one line, but has hidden depths and layers.
That we swim from feeling lost, lonely, *sola y perdida*,
mistaking passing states of percolating in perjury for
permanence
while an unseen root of joy and gems germinates
in the earth of the aftermath of each *despedida*.
To emerge into newness: *así es la vida*
turning us from jet streams into warmer orbits,
mitigating pain with waves of love, *con olas de amor*.
Estas aguas, muddy and blurred, will clear:
Their expanse not something to fear – *pero un mundo entero*,
a whole world to explore
even with you not here.

To breathe is *respirar…* like taking respite

Like letting your soul rest, and knowing the resplendence of light

That comes in the wake of things ended,

Attesting to restoration, that wounds become mended,

strength grown making strokes in currents of independence.

Como este camino aumenta tu fortaleza, tu fuerza,

A fortress wrought within rapids of sadness,

a core of truth found at the heart of *tristeza.*

All you can do is trust when you can't see through the mist;

solo vés lo que falta

When you just see what's missed.

When life's sound is like a language I don't understand

and my landmarks are drowned in the past – things we planned

–

aunque no lo veo, me voy hacia la tierra

Even though I can't see it, I'm heading for dry land

Mi pena desvanece, my sorrow disappears,

with the marks of my pen

todo hecho a mano, slow work done by hand,

again and again

creando nuevos castillos,

alcanzando la tierra:

building new castles,

reaching the sand.

(Y)our light continuing…

Nature's with us as we stretch out
to feel energised and powerful.
I'm drinking up our time together, taking sips from each hour
full,
Swept away by new weather: external storms colliding,
coinciding, syncing up with our pull towards each other.
Your eyes draw me into worlds that we've yet to uncover,
their gold and green holding me – an invitation to explore
something delicious, supercharged, warm.
You say that our souls have met somewhere before
and I feel like life's shifting to take on new forms
As you break down my norms
As you rotate shapes in our shared landscapes,
Like the days are countdowns until you're rotating shapes on my
body -
Until I'm tight in your embrace with no will to escape
Until I'm rivers of sweat blessing the skin of your face….
Splaying out feelings, impossibly raw.

What's being a person for if not this?

Treading the borders between fear and bliss;

At the same time that I have you, I'm hungry for more.

Your not-giving-a-fuck-ness:

It's infectious,

A purple force field that swells to protect us

dislodging me from vibrations of stodginess and feeling-stuck-

ness

daydreaming about evenings of your words and touches.

Is this all too much? Is this a danger to discard familiar crutches?

Like poems,

Cause now language just seems like it's cheapening

To minutes and moments of our energy deepening.

Like these bodies are temporary roles adopted by souls who have

an eternal alliance;

Only you can explain the insane using science,

Only you can I talk with when we're sat in still silence

Burning with tenderness laced with dashes and sharp thrills of
violence.

Don't hang on to my read receipts,

These words are yours to keep

Part of a circle whose light stream is endless

Whose orbit's extending

Cycles of cutting ourselves open and mending.

You're everything – maybe – apart from pretending.

You say you wanna get out so that we can live free.

It must be happening already, because I've never felt more like
me.

Working title: Healing

The journey to Ealing
never looked this appealing;
You tore down my defences
like that storm ripped down fences
Exposed the soft raw part of me
locked tight in the heart of me
That they've spent a quarter-century concealing and trying not to
mention -
protected by pretension and a terror of revealing.
It's shifting beyond my conscious comprehension
like the teenage rewiring of the prefrontal cortex,
There's joy and pain coalesced in a vortex,
and a page can't contain all the things that I'm feeling,
all my atoms congealing.

When you break through the doors to the pathway of healing
you feel all your flaws,
and it can't be done halfway:

you're back to the Source, to the Cause,

to impressions you've always known but weren't allowed to be

yours,

to a new-born infant, squealing and screaming,

a place you've visited before in nightmares and dreaming.

'Cause it's deep in your core,

trapped in ice that's starting to thaw

and its power leaves you reeling, too true to ignore.

This is the hour: it's squaring you in the face,

all this newfound space, the past finally airing,

and it shakes all your bearings.

The hurt of it cuts like a knife,

but for the first time in your life,

your wings are preparing to soar.

Keep your feet firm on the floor as you fly.

We need anchors on Earth while our souls float the sky;

Icarus learnt how we melt if riding too high,

his body a boat-hull keeling, boy-voice sending bird-cries

keening,

drifted too far from a safe berth,

feathers like the tatters of tether-less kites…

It's being seen and heard to matter in the light of our worth

that gives our flights meaning.

The sun is so bright that I'm kneeling, knocked over,

face-first into fields full of four-leafed clovers,

going gentle while weaning myself off of these memories,

their colours Catherine-wheeling

past where my scattered selves are reconvening,

from the time they've been stealing.

When I come to find you on Windmill Road,

will my presence remind you of karma we're both owed?

Can we nurture these bodies when they carry loads?

They say trauma can blind you when stirred

from the caverns in muscles that it's spent years stowed,

like then and now become blurred in our tears,

recalling the imprint of disinterred fears.

This was a ticking-bomb that was only ever bound to explode.

Unsure how long aftershock waves will stay ringing,

my words and the sound of your singing are only half-heard

when its twinges come stinging.

Like gunshots slinging have left us dumbfounded,

grappling and floundering to get grounded

every second seeming slowed.

I am astounded by this frequency of love,

like amniotic fluid of music, psalms pealing,

coating us surrounded while we're falling, sprawling over each
other,

on top of the covers, mere marks on the maps of our ancestors,

shvitzing and spieling.

I reverberate aglow in a new mode, drink the warmth that you're
bringing,

in the lap of this life to relax and to sink.

Our eyes have their own code, and its growth has no ceiling.

Splay time

We splay

our clothes　　　our stuff　　　our selves

all over the floor, eschewing hangers and shelves.

We say

we'll clear up: fold　　sort　　stack...

But some words hurt so much that they can't be put back -

Just leaving you gasping

trying to find a patch of　　uncluttered　　space　　amongst

everything strewn

trying to re-wind to a well-known place

rendered hostile in the harsh sun of an alien afternoon.

Like the dark side of the moon,

marked by mirrors and traps;

You said together we would heal

but this feels like collapse.

If we tidy up soon, how long before relapse?

Lost in landscapes for which they've invented no maps.

I don't think I've ever met two people with such phenomenal

superpowers

for turning bedrooms to bombsites in minutes or hours

where churned-up soil leaves scant space for flowers.

Something once unspoilt now recoils and cowers,

part of me so scared, as if watched by panopticon towers

where you're never sure which way guards' eyes are angled.

We're adept it taking cleanness, leaving it mangled;

our garments like our karma, separate yet entangled.

Now it seems we share scars

like the night sky bears stars:

the canvas on which our own lifespans are spangled.

We'll work this scrubland - it's time to replant,

But I know that there's things that won't heal with a chant.

The process of extracting Who We Are from what we aren't

returning crumpled shirts, socks, skirts, to cupboard drawers.

Can my eyes still discern what's mine from what's yours?

For now, they can, but what happens when they can't?

Dank green smoke screen

Half-sat, half-lying relaxed in the hammock at the back of your
garden,
Caught between laptop-eyeing and looking skywards
Your gaze glazed over under lazed-out eyelids with a layer of
sheen and shine,
Indicative of your mind winding, climbing to a place where
everything seems like a sign
and music's polyrhythmic pace intertwines with shadows of
concurrent thoughts that you're running to chase
mirroring sunlight flecks falling onto my face in divinely
ordained alignment.
Thoughts become geometries in quantities measured exact;
and all is more beautiful but it's harder to act, 'cause moving
and doing things becomes like a really high-level assignment
making it easier to stay in computer game land, AKA solo
confinement.
Summer in the suburbs – quiet but never silent,
Lolling in the lull of this half-stagnated climate.

This weather – it's sticky and green which feels pretty apt

For you coating yourself in an inhaled haze,

Smiling from behind the smoke screen as if muffled in a carpet

of snow,

this daze in which you're wrapped.

The green swirls greyness and scent and curls her tendrils

around you

birdsong mixing with Heathrow distant jet-fuel sound, you

press one of my hands against the dank green wall of our

relationship's maze

as the other of yours plays with the hem of my dress.

Both our eyes are ablaze while I slowly forget all the ways back

to the entrance/exit door,

Lack of balance, eardrums dizzying more,

now my grip's lost the edge and I find myself bruised on the

floor

knowing that you're stronger

no longer sure of the moment when something snapped

and this game that's a joy to explore became a space where

you're trapped,

Spun backwards, pushed down,

Grappling to breathe through a face full of ground.

I wonder what parts of you

this dank green smoke screen is stopping me from knowing,

And whether it's you or the draws that I'm talking to when

you're forgetful and confused

Or how to get through when you speak with illusion and start

accusing me,

Is it grounds for dispute or THC leaves at the root? Truth or

paranoia?

Refreshment or rotten fruit encased in each zoot?

This tool, this creator of imagination, is also a destroyer:

a straitjacket and deployer of knee-jerk reactions

and obsessive reflection, nit-picking, dissection of my actions

while we flick from unity into mimicry of warring factions,

words that stick against past wounds, gaining traction.

I love you with my heart's totality, regardless of how you treat

me.

Both slaves to the stars, lost in our shared reality.

Yeah, what's the difference between a few emotional scars and the games that we play where you beat me?

Beat and delete, fuck and chuck, hump and dump

But I can't bear to leave - the thought floods my lungs with a lump

And each time we make up from threats to break up the love flows so sweetly.

In our own stasis, sipping the waters of a private oasis and they say that time heals

but it never erases.

Part of me still shakes even while the tension dissipates,

and I hear it all again in flashback reels, with no option to pause, every syllable grating.

If I am caught waiting to become more yours than the emeralds which lurk in plastic baggies of draws

how long will I be vying for your trust before I give up hope?

I need you know that this isn't a cuss,

We all do what we must to cope,

Descendants of dust, sucking in sustenance, gasping as we pray
not to choke,

never far from the cusp.

Days in the cloud of your smoke lose their lustre

and the love that you promised would be everlasting has left

my throat rasping,

lungs tightened and closed while I stutter and cut my heart

open

'Cause I've breathed for you all of the air I can muster

and get left with the ends, a bouquet of extinguished butts,

The times you've put me down, treated me as your slut,

leaving marks of invisible burns,

claiming your mind's so open when it's really so shut,

Only accepts moving forwards if I do so on your terms.

Then you come back with puppy dog eyes as if your mouth

wouldn't melt butter

Look at me like you know how to, to make my insides flutter.

You say anything so you feel safe, and now these hugs start to

feel like they chafe,

a faraway cry from the fantasies you sold

while you morph me and scold, try to melt me to fit your

subservient mould,

voice turned distant and cold,

so certain that you've got the world sussed.

Can you tell me the difference between your love and your lust?

In each vice-like hold, I feel growing disgust with your denial of

my hurt.

The expectations that I serve every rule you assert,

Triggers firing vitriol like bullets to swerve.

Take your lighter to my feelings; toss their ashes to the gutter,

Demote me from equal to item of clutter,

left to dirty, disused.

You think this a bluff, or some kind of ruse?

This time, you don't get to choose.

I refuse to rot in this rut and watch your respect for me rust.

Time to follow the knowledge that nests in my gut

that I cannot stay put.

My legs feel like jelly

but I know in my core, they still remember how to stand up.

So I'm getting clean, 'cause my skin shade's never suited green,

You can find someone else to control and demean.

I might cough and splutter while I leave, but my way moves

into fresh air,

away from the mines which litter the field of your care.

Live in your lonely dream-world, trauma sprinkled with a

surface layer of glitter

stoned out of your mind posting bullshit on Twitter.

My way through is to discard being bitter

but you make cordiality hard when your final move is criticism.

It's a schism.

Yeah, I've given and given, and it isn't enough

done my best to explain I don't thrive when restrained

and I need to survive outside cuffs and chains.

A house made of rizla falls down with one puff

and this love's been struck at by gust after gust.

My resources are drained.

Rest tight in your hammock, seeking help from the skies;

I can only give this thing so many tries.

Soft boy ranting

Beware men who proclaim "I stand with the oppressed,"
but command and chastise you while you get undressed,
Sure that they can do no wrong, because they've clearly expressed
that they're feminists and act to serve minority groups' interests.

Read *Why Does He Do That?* by Lundy Bancroft
'Cause abuse hits hard, but abusers can be soft boys who feel deep and tell you their fears,
who've picked up healing jargon from being in therapy for years.
Then in arguments, he tears you down with icy ripostes –
Once he's made up his mind, you've already lost
gaslighting 'til you're certain that it's your wires that are crossed.
You can stay with this man, but ask yourself: at what cost?

On social issues, he always takes the admirable stance,

But he also takes the floor so no-one else gets a chance.

Happy up on a high horse of ethics and morality,

vision blinkered from the harm that he seeds in reality.

Whether it's his trauma or the weather, there's always some

excuse

for how he scolds and undermines you, but he doesn't see it as

abuse –

In fact, he thinks that *you're* the one who's infringing on *his*

rights.

Didn't you learn that it should be the man who gets the final say

in fights?

And he who decides when we start, when we stop, controls the

pace –

He's cut you too much slack – now he'll put you back in your

place.

He can cut you down with insults or a condescending tone.

And you share a bed and share your lives, but really, you're

alone.

His anger flares and scares you, but yours is never permitted, so you keep your comebacks silent and head down, smiling

though your teeth are gritted,

Remembering how you fell in love and those first doubts that

flitted;

Now that love is mixed with danger, and it pains you to admit

it.

Maybe you are the crazy one, because you feel messed up and

skittish.

But it's stiff upper lip and a cuppa, 'cause what can I say? I'm

British.

Don't share opinions, for the Truth is his turf,

A million papercuts, erasing your sense of self-worth.

I bent myself and bled for you, so eager to fucking please

But all the tears and sweat I shed for you reduced me to my

knees.

Until I was begging you to listen

and all you did was mock me,

with every sneer and each derision,

our safe space became a prison,

whose aftermath still shocks me.

It hurts me – all that I couldn't convey –

shouting, screaming 'til this throat is sore

stuffing un-seaming from my insides

and collecting in pools on the floor.

Every line I write or blurt set to fall onto deaf ears,

walled out by the palace of denial that you've built yourself

over the years.

I'm sad that after all we shared, its structure stays the same.

Moat prepared for someone new to grow ensnared within your

game.

Repeat the dance of barbed-wire love which once was home to

me.

I'm free, but my landscape remains landmarked:

its liberty littered with debris.

Seeds

(The product of dating someone in an open relationship)

Watch out for those seeds, girl, those seeds in your mind,

because he'll move on and you'll get left behind -

Maybe it isn't just love, but lust too, that's blind,

and these rules to adjust to leave you feeling resigned.

It turns on yet disgusts you - your place, second-best -

Permitted to share passion but not to share rest,

Stone-set, no matter how much you've expressed

that you only want equal – not slapped down to "less".

'Cause your heart's on the line, but for him, it's just sport

And it's your body not your intellect that occupies his thoughts.

He rains showers of deep talking, edges blur and distort,

You're sleep-walking – to wake up in spider webs caught.

Do you like how it feels, to make me your whore?

Reminds me of when he asked me to sleep on his floor

'cause he didn't want me in his bed any more

so I came to meet you, already bruised and sore.

Your seat is like the throne of ultimate choice,

you can switch on my moans, and switch off my voice.

Tell me in half-joking tones "be careful of those seeds,"

that you helped to plant too, that you knew would sprout

weeds.

I'll hack down all their fruits – I can do this alone,

If their roots prove too tough, he'll go back to his throne.

Not compliant enough – I was costly to own –

so the apps can procure another dolly girl-shaped clone.

I leave the wintery earth churned-up and barren and still

to take care of myself. Always have, always will.

New Friend

I think maybe that we're insane in the same ways,

adept at pouring balm on those places where pain stays.

Breathing in, stretching out, recovering day by day –

growth-bound, even if the madness never fully goes away.

Looking for self-love

I don't know how to face

The   empty   space

The sleeping and waking alone,

6 a.m. shivers, when I turn to my phone

Like pixels rearranging themselves

In all the right ways to addict me

is the best use of my gaze,

Brightness burning a hole in sleep,

combing through pictures of men who've – *yay* – picked me

to be their one-night plaything or piece on the side.

Exciting, enticing, yet rings hollow quickly

In hours where my self-doubt has nowhere to hide.

Wounds barely stitched up, running deeper than I'd known,

against whose stings these text-flirts sing in cheaper tones.

I swing my fingers like protective shields across this screen

making drumbeat patterns of tapping the glass

bathe my scars in electronic field.

I'll do anything to stop mapping the past,

rallentando rhythms rattling to make solo hours pass.

And I grasp without fire at the traces of things

as if shopping-cart flings

could be suitable stuffing to fill out the gap that you left,

or could calm down the racing and pains in my chest.

But attempts to replace scraped-out flesh with cotton wool

leave my heart feeling more vacant than full.

I'm scared of the darkness that gapes

where my mind's a cinema replaying old tapes

and I'm flicking switches, fumbling, at a loss for how to turn the

light on.

I think maybe it's **me** that I need to swipe right on.

Say yes, I accept you, you're welcome in my world,

and I honour this connection, nurture it to unfurl

and you look great today even though you're tired.

Magnetise towards wavelengths that render you inspired –

discerning the difference between being respected and desired.

I'm proud to hold you when the future's unclear:

when you yearn to belong, when your body holds fear.

I've seen how you're strong, caring and kind;

watched the nights turning over weights within the mind,

searching uncertain for scattered soul pieces

seeking deeper rest than saccharine releases.

You make out victory's cadence between bars of daily grind,

ever dancing onwards through a life you can't rewind,

daring to hear hopefulness in mundane footfall sounds:

music in the rhythm struck each time they hit the ground.

I open space for you to grow and feel your way

refresh your eyes with colour when vision's painted grey,

stoke fires of self-compassion and keep their light kindled

through romances which come and go, those flames which

blaze then dwindle.

The sunrise dawns, half-blindingly –

a need for love's been blinding me.

My thoughts like sparks, unwinding free,

breaking down to breakthrough, fusion from fission.

Light of pages and their open lines

dim out the dark to let me shine:

a snowdrop in mud, a silent mission.

Acknowledgements

Thank you for taking the time to read my poetry – and for getting to the last page. Many thanks to the talented and resourceful Natàlia Pàmies Lluís for designing this pamphlet's cover artwork. A huge and ongoing thank you to my family and friends for always being an encouraging audience for my writing and performance, and whose love and laughter is a constant source of nourishment. I am grateful to those who have inspired and fed my passion for literature: teachers, professors, and all who courageously share their own creativity while fostering space for others to do the same.